D0366490

SPRINT Edition

★ SPORTS STARS ★

MARION JONES

SPRINTING SENSATION

BY MARK STEWART

SCHOLASTIC INC.
New York Toronto London Auckland Sydney
Mexico City New Delhi Hong Kong Buenos Aires

Photo Credits
Cover: Rob Tringali Jr.; Title Page: © Gray Mortimore/AllSport/Getty Images; p. 6: © Gray Mortimore/AllSport/Getty Images; p. 10: © Tony Duffy/AllSport/Getty Images; p. 13: © Mike Powell/AllSport/Getty Images; p. 14: © Al Bello/AllSport/Getty Images; p. 17: © Many Millan/Sports Illustrated Picture Collection; p. 18: © Tony Duffy/All Sport/Getty Images; p. 21: © Doug Pensinger/AllSport/Getty Images; p. 25: © University of North Carolina Athletic Communications; p. 26: © Gary Hershorn/Reuters; p. 28: © Eric Risberg/AP/Wide World Photos; p. 29: © Stephen Dunn/AllSport/Getty Images; p. 31: © Mike Powell/AllSport/Getty Images; p. 32: © Gary Hershorn/Reuters/Getty Images; p. 35: © Al Bello/AllSport/Getty Images; p. 36: © Mark Thompson/AllSport/Getty Images; p. 40: © Michael Probst/AP/WideWorld Photos; p. 43: Bongarts Photography/SportsChrome; p. 44 tl: © Tony Duffy/All Sport/Getty Images, tr: © Mike Powell/All Sport/Getty Images; p. 45: tr: © Michael Probst/AP/WideWorld Photos p. 45: tl: © Mark Thompson/AllSport/Getty Images, tr: © p. 46: © Agence France Presse/CORBIS; p. 47: © Mike Powell/AllSport/Getty Images.

Published by Scholastic Inc., 557 Broadway,
New York, NY 10012.
Printed in the U.S.A.

ISBN 0-516-27733-2

1 2 3 4 5 6 7 8 9 10 61 12 11 10 09 08 07 06 05 04 03

CONTENTS

160
TRACK & FIELD
CHAMPIONSHIPS

1

GO AHEAD, SMILE

A loud roar from the crowd washes over Marion Jones as she breaks the tape. Far in front of the other runners, she peers up at her time. She tries her best to look serious, but it's a struggle. The fans are still cheering her victory. As soon as she glances into the stands, she cannot help herself. Her face relaxes. Then a little smile begins. Finally, she cracks her trademark grin. The cheers grow even louder. If you look closer, you'll see that the fans are also smiling back at Marion. This champion clearly enjoys her fans' love. And she gives it right back to them.

☆ ☆ ☆

It takes a lot of personality to light up an entire stadium with a smile. Legends like Magic Johnson and Olga Korbut had it. Baseball star Sammy Sosa has it, too. But few track stars have been able to connect with fans in this way. Marion has everything an athlete could ask for. She has talent, grace, and a competitive spirit. And she has a great outlook. “As long as you’re running fast,” she often says, “life is good.”

No wonder she is smiling. She has been running faster and jumping longer than any woman in history.

2

ALWAYS ON THE RUN

Marion Jones was not like most of the other little girls in her town. "I had no use for dolls or any girl things," she says. "Or even girlfriends." She was always looking for a challenge. She liked to hang around with her older brother, Albert, and his friends. Marion also tested her mother and stepfather at every turn. She'd go head to head with anyone over anything. The other kids called Marion "Hard Nails" because she was so tough.

Marion's parents decided not to punish her or try to control her. Instead, they directed Marion's incredible energy toward sports. She played tee ball, softball, and basketball. She did gymnastics,

Marion Jones was already a track star in high school.

ran track, and even took ballet and tap-dancing lessons. She was always on the go. "The only time I'd come in was to grab a piece of fruit and go to the bathroom," she claims.

When Marion was in the sixth grade, her stepfather died. She and Ira were very close, and she was deeply saddened by the loss. After he died, things got tough. Marion's mother sometimes had to work two jobs to support the family. Inspired by her mother, Marion worked harder than ever. She pushed herself in the

☆ ☆ ☆

classroom and on the playing fields. She was already the national track champion in her age group. And she was becoming quite a basketball player as well.

Marion's mother knew her daughter would do great things. So she moved the family three times in four years. The idea was to get Marion into the best schools for both academics and sports. Her plan worked. Marion blossomed into a great runner. She was best at short runs, or sprints. In 10th grade, Marion recorded the season's fastest times in the 100, 200, and 400 meters.

In high school, Marion became one of the top basketball players in the Los Angeles area. She continued to dominate in track, too. As a junior she recorded the six best times in the country at 100 meters. She also recorded the nine fastest times at 200 meters.

Marion made it to the 1992 Olympic trials, but she just missed qualifying for the 200 meters. Still, she earned a spot on the U.S. relay team as an alternate. She was just 16 years old. Then she

☆ ☆ ☆

stunned everyone by quitting the Olympic team. Here's why. Alternates would get medals if the team won. They'd even get a medal *if they didn't run.* Marion didn't want to get her first Olympic medal that way. "When I get my first medal," she said, "I want to have earned it, sweated for it."

Marion ended up watching the Olympics on television. It was frustrating. So, she took her frustration out on the basketball court. It was her senior year, and what a season she had! Marion finished her high school basketball career averaging 22.8 points and 14.7 rebounds a game. She was named California High School Player of the Year. Her team had a two-year record of 60–4. They had reached the state championship game both years.

When spring came, Marion was back on track, literally. She again won sprint after sprint. She also became interested in the long jump for the first time.

In her first meet, she jumped 19' 10 3/4". Three weeks later she improved to 20' 9 1/4". At the California High School Championships, she jumped 22' 1/2". That was enough to win the meet. It was

Marion strains to make the team at the 1992 U.S. Olympic Trials.

Marion jumps at the 1993 California state championships. She came within three inches of setting a U.S. record.

☆ ☆ ☆

also just three inches short of a new national record. This jump locked up her third straight National Player of the Year Award.

College scholarship offers were arriving almost daily. Marion's athletic skill and excellent grades meant she could go anywhere. Marion was interested in becoming a writer, and the University of North Carolina (UNC) had a terrific journalism department. But she didn't want to choose between basketball and track. "I figured I'd do both," she explains. UNC agreed. Her mother liked the school, too. One last thing settled it. "In the beginning I needed discipline," Marion remembers. "And the Carolina basketball program is very structured."

TAR HEEL TERROR

Marion arrived at UNC in 1993. She met with basketball coach Sylvia Hatchell. Coach Hatchell asked her if she would switch from forward to point guard. At 5'10", Marion was used to playing on the front court. Becoming a "floor general" was something new. Coach Hatchell thought the team was thin at point guard. She believed that Marion's incredible speed would be useful at this position. She could pressure opponents into mistakes that would create easy baskets. Marion agreed to try it. After just four games, she took over the starting point guard job.

Marion (20) and her Tar Heel teammates celebrate their 1994 national championship.

Marion competes in the long jump at the 1994 NCAA Track and Field Championships. She placed second.

☆ ☆ ☆

The UNC Tar Heels had a good team. Marion made it better. At the beginning of the season, they were ranked about ninth or tenth in the nation. Once Marion started running the floor, the team lost just two games all year. In the 1994 NCAA Tournament, the Tar Heels made it to the championship game. There they faced two-time champion Louisiana Tech. With one second left, UNC was behind 59–57. Then UNC teammate Charlotte Smith hit a three-pointer. It won them the national championship! Although Smith got the headlines, Marion played a big part in making it happen. Her cool-headed play and great passing kept the Tar Heels close for much of the game.

While her teammates were still celebrating, Marion had to switch gears. She moved directly into track season, and what a season it was. She earned All-America honors in four track and field events.

☆ ☆ ☆

Marion was named co-captain of the basketball team her sophomore year. The UNC Tar Heels went on to have another fabulous season. They won the Atlantic Coast Conference (ACC) championship for the second consecutive time. UNC was denied a shot at another national championship, however. They were upset by George Washington University in the NCAA Tournament.

Just as she had done the year before, Marion went straight from basketball to track. Again she earned All-America honors. Still, she felt she hadn't done her best. Playing two sports didn't allow her to focus. Also, her "basketball body" was holding her back. She was a dozen pounds heavier than her ideal sprinting weight. "I tried to tune out track and field," she remembers. "That was the easiest way to get through it for me, but the love never died." And Marion did not like to do things halfway.

Marion runs the show as the UNC point guard. Eventually, she had to choose between basketball and track.

☆ ☆ ☆

During the summer of 1995, Marion began to dream about the Olympics. They were a year away. She was certain she could make the U.S. track or basketball squad. The question was, which one? Marion chose track, but first she wanted to play in one last basketball tournament—the World University Games. At the tryouts, disaster struck! Marion broke her ankle. To speed her recovery, doctors inserted two metal screws into the bone. There was still a chance it would heal in time for the Olympics. After a brief rest, she began training again, but while jumping on a trampoline, her ankle turned and the screws bent. That ended her chance to be in the Olympics. Marion was devastated. Just as she had four years earlier, Marion watched the Summer Games on television.

The next season, Marion returned to the basketball court healthy and focused. Once again, the Tar Heels took the ACC title. Unfortunately, they also lost again in the NCAA Tournament.

☆ ☆ ☆

Marion had averaged 18.1 points per game over three seasons. During that time, the team lost just ten games. Marion could still play for one more year. But she decided it was time to move on. She had finished her journalism studies. She felt her basketball and track skills would be wasted if she stayed. It was time for her to step up to the next level. It was time to choose between two sports she loved.

☆ 4 ☆

BACK ON TRACK

Most people assumed that Marion would join a women's pro basketball team. At the time, there were two pro leagues: the American Basketball League (ABL) and Women's National Basketball Association (WNBA). Both were fighting to sign the best players. Salaries were going through the roof. Marion was quite a catch. She was the fastest player in the women's game. She could also dunk. But when it came time to decide, Marion followed her heart. "I chose track," she says. "It was always my first love."

There was another reason Marion's heart was set on track. His name was C.J. Hunter.

All the pro basketball teams wanted Marion.

Marion's coach, Trevor Graham, is a former sprinter from Jamaica.

☆ ☆ ☆

Marion met C.J. when he was a strength coach at UNC. Hunter was also a famous shot-putter. They struck up a close friendship. It quickly grew into a romance. By 1996, they were spending almost all of their time together. However, Hunter wasn't the only important man in her life. C.J. introduced Marion to his coach, Trevor Graham. Graham watched Marion run for a few minutes. Then he made a couple of simple suggestions. "Trevor changed little things, like the angle of my blocks or the way I carried one arm, and I improved immediately," she remembers.

Graham saw that Marion's greatest asset was not her body. It was her head. She liked to break things down and analyze them. For instance, Marion knew that a sprint was more than a single burst of energy. It was a "set of strides" that could be worked on and improved. This made her very easy to coach. The two also discussed her long jumping at great length. Graham convinced Marion to try a completely different style. She mastered it after just a couple of minutes.

Marion could beat the records set by Florence Griffith-Joyner more than a decade ago.

In 1997, Marion burst into the national spotlight at the U.S. Track and Field Championships. The timing was perfect. People in the sport had been worried. There were no up-and-coming American stars to attract new fans, especially among the women. A decade earlier, Florence Griffith-Joyner had brought glamour and excitement to track. Incredible athletes like

Gail Devers, Gwen Torrence, and Jackie Joyner-Kersee kept the flame alive through the 1990s. Who would take their place in the next decade?

As if to answer, Marion stepped up and ran the 100-meter semifinal in 10.92 seconds. Marion who? The fans began looking for their programs. Only a handful of women had ever run that fast before. In the final, she was so far ahead that she slowed down the last ten meters or so. Still, she turned in an incredible time of 10.97 seconds!

Marion's idol is Jackie Joyner-Kersee.

☆ ☆ ☆

Next was the long jump. Jackie Joyner-Kersee owned this event. She was going for her eighth straight national title. She was unbeatable. Then Marion stepped up to the line. A sprinter *and* a long jumper? Who was this woman?

The fans cheered for the underdog as Marion powered her way into the lead, but Joyner-Kersee battled right back. She regained the lead on her fifth and final jump. It was not the first time the 35-year-old legend had put down a young challenger.

Marion was not intimidated. She calmly got up, and chugged down the runway. She launched her body into the air. Her jump was 22' 9". That was one inch longer than Joyner-Kersee's. It was good enough to make Marion the new national champion.

Next Marion set her sights on the 1997 World Championships. It was a major international event. That summer she flew to Athens, Greece. How would a newcomer perform in such an

Marion competes in the 100 meters at the 1997 World Championships in Greece.

important meet? Would she choke? One thing was for sure. She would be tested. In the second round of the 100-meter race, there was a delay. It lasted for an hour. The other runners paced anxiously and complained, but Marion stayed cool. But the test wasn't over. The finals began

Marion (left) flexes her muscles with 4 x 100 teammates Gail Devers, Inger Miller, and Chryste Gaines.

☆ ☆ ☆

with a false start. The runners had to wait for three long minutes for the signal. Again, Marion kept her cool. When the starter's pistol fired, she rocketed out of the blocks. She streaked across the finish line with a winning time of 10.83 seconds. That victory gave Marion her first taste of gold, and she wanted more. She got it as a member of the 4 x 100 relay team. She was the only woman to win two gold medals at the meet. Marion showed that she was no flash in the pan.

Marion continued her rise to superstardom. She won events and fans all over the world in 1997. That fall, she was voted best in her sport. Most people thought it would be impossible for her to top that honor. Well, they were wrong.

5

ALMOST PERFECT

Marion kicked off her 1998 season with victories in the 100 and 200 meters at meets in Australia. Then she competed in Japan, winning an indoor 60-meter race. After that, Marion returned to the United States, where she won the long jump at a North Carolina track meet. In April, she traveled to California and won a 400-meter competition. Then she traveled east to the Penn Relays. There she crossed the tape in the final leg of the 4 x 200 meters. Things got even busier in May. Marion won sprints in Japan and China. She jumped 23' 11 3/4" at a meet in Oregon. This was a new personal best.

At the U.S. Track and Field Championships in June, Marion did what no one had done in 50 years. She won the gold in the 100 and 200 meters and the long jump. After the meet, people

Marion sprints to victory in the 100 meters at the 1998 Goodwill Games.

were calling her the sport's greatest athlete ever. Jackie Joyner-Kersee, who would retire that summer, had long held that title. Marion was not so sure she was ready to replace her idol. "I don't deserve the title," she says. "I still consider Jackie the best female athlete, and probably always will."

Marion catches her breath at the 1998 IAAF World Cup, where she won gold in the 100 and 200 meters.

After the nationals, Marion went to Europe for the summer track tour. There she won every event she entered. In July, she returned briefly to the United States to compete in the Goodwill Games. At the games, she won gold medals in the 100 and 200 meters.

Marion's final meet in 1998 came in Johannesburg, South Africa. She competed in the International Amateur Athletic Federation (IAAF) World Cup. Marion was in peak form. She won the 100 meters in 10.49 seconds and the 200 meters in 21.34 seconds. Each of these marks represented the second-fastest times in the history of the sport. Then Marion lost in the long jump; it was her first loss that season.

While in South Africa, Marion had a very moving experience. She visited the country's all-black Soweto township. She learned, to her surprise, that she was considered a great hero and inspiration to the people there. Not long ago, black athletes were not allowed to compete in

☆ ☆ ☆

South Africa. "The Soweto experience was incredible," Marion says. "We train so much, we travel so much, we do so many meets, we sometimes forget about what is really important. That put things into perspective for me. There are people out there who have to live hard-core lives every day they wake up."

Marion's 1998 season was truly something to behold. When it was all over, she had entered 37 events and won 36. She competed in six different events, winning the gold in every one. Her one loss, in the long jump, had come on a track that was wet and slick from rain.

6

THE OLYMPICS AND BEYOND

In 1999, Marion cut back her schedule. She wanted to gear up for the World Championships in Seville, Spain. She also wanted to enjoy life as a newlywed. She and C.J. had gotten married in the fall of 1998.

But bad luck struck in Seville. Marion hurt her back while competing for gold medals in four events. She needed a rest. Her focus now was the 2000 Olympics in Sydney, Australia. She had a goal for herself. She wanted to win five Olympic gold medals. No other track athlete had ever done it.

Marion celebrates her first of five medals at the Sydney Olympics.

☆ ☆ ☆

The press couldn't stop talking about Marion's quest. Lots of people were rooting for her, but not everyone. Said one rival, "It shouldn't be as if no one else is even competing in her races. It's not like Marion Jones is Superwoman and everyone else is poultry."

When Marion arrived in Sydney in the fall of 2000, the pressure was on. Would she get her five gold medals? Her chances were good. She won her first race, the 100 meters, by the second biggest margin in Olympic history. That was one gold down, four to go.

Marion got two more gold medals. They came in the 200 meters and the 4 x 400-meter relay. She got bronze medals in both the long jump and the 4 x 100-meter relay. That made her the first female track-and-field athlete to win five medals at a single Olympics. They weren't all gold, but it was still impressive, and she emerged as the top female sprinter in the world. The press named her Athlete of the Year.

☆ ☆ ☆

The next two seasons saw major changes in Marion's life. In 2001, she split up with C.J. And she left her coach, Trevor Graham, in 2002, but none of this slowed her down. In 2001 she won a gold medal in the 200 meters at the World Championships. In 2002, she won another gold medal at the World Championships, this time in the 100 meters. In fact, she didn't lose a single race during 2002. She became the first American athlete in seven years to have an undefeated season. For that, Marion received her third Jesse Owens Award, U.S. track and field's highest honor.

Marion wants to become the fastest woman in history. Her goal is to break sprinting records in the 100 and 200 meters. She also wants to set records in the long jump. "Before my career is over, I will attempt to run faster than any woman has ever run and jump farther than any woman has ever jumped," she says. Fans are rooting for her. If anyone can do it, Marion can, and she'll do it with a smile.

Marion may never let up, but she knows how to relax and enjoy the success that she has achieved.

C ☆ H ☆ R ☆ O ☆ N

1975	• Oct. 12: Marion is born in Los Angeles, California.
1981	• Marion begins competing in track-and-field events during grade school.
1986	• Marion joins her first organized basketball league.
1991	• Marion wins her first of three National Player of the Year awards for girls' track.
1993	• Marion is named California's top high school basketball player.
1994	• Marion leads the University of North Carolina to the NCAA basketball championship, which they win.
1995	• Injury keeps Marion out of the 1996 Olympics; she chooses track and field over basketball.
1997	• Marion becomes the U.S. and world champion in the 100 meters, and the U.S. champion in the long jump.

1998 • Marion wins 36 out of 37 national and international track-and-field events.

1999 • Marion becomes the world champion in the 100 meters; a back injury keeps her out for the rest of the season.

2000 • Marion wins five medals at the Sydney Olympics: a gold in the 100 meters, 200 meters, and 4 x 400-meter relay, and a bronze in the long jump and the 4 x 100-meter relay. She is the first female athlete to win five medals at a single Olympics.

2001 • Marion becomes the world champion in the 200 meters; she also becomes a ten-time U.S. Outdoor Champion.

2002 • Marion has the first undefeated season of her career. She wins a gold medal in the 100 meters at the World Championships.

1160

★ HONORS AND CHAMPIONSHIPS ★

National High School Player of the Year (Track) 1991, 1992, 1993
California High School Player of the Year (Basketball) 1993
NCAA Women's Basketball Champion, 1994
NCAA Track & Field All-American, 1994, 1995
NCAA Basketball All-American, 1997
World 100 Meters Champion, 1997, 1999, 2002
World 200 Meters Champion, 2001
Track & Field Athlete of the Year, 1997, 1998, 2000, 2002
National Long Jump Champion, 1997, 1998
National 100 Meters Champion, 1997, 1998, 2002
National 200 Meters Champion, 1997, 1998, 1999, 2001, 2002
Goodwill Games Gold Medalist, 1998, 2001, 2002
Jesse Owens Award Winner, 1997, 1998, 2002

ABOUT THE AUTHOR

Mark Stewart has written hundreds of features and more than fifty books about sports for young readers. A nationally syndicated columnist ("Mark My Words"), he lives and works in New Jersey. For Children's Press, Stewart is the author of more than twenty books in the Sports Stars series, including biographies of other women athletes such as Lisa Leslie, Monica Seles, and Mia Hamm. He is also the author of the Watts History of Sports, a six-volume history of auto racing, baseball, basketball, football, hockey, and soccer.